In loving memory of my grandad, John Featherstone,
who instilled my love of storytelling – R.D.

For Joshua – M.B.

Published in the UK by Scholastic, 2024
1 London Bridge, London, SE1 9BG
Scholastic Ireland, 89E Lagan Road, Dublin Industrial Estate,
Glasnevin, Dublin, D11 HP5F

SCHOLASTIC and associated logos are trademarks and/or
registered trademarks of Scholastic Inc.

Text © Rachael Davis, 2024
Illustrations © Mike Byrne, 2024

The right of Rachael Davis and Mike Byrne to be identified
as the author and illustrator of this work has been asserted by them
under the Copyright, Designs and Patents Act 1988.

PB ISBN 978 0702 31844 3

A CIP catalogue record for this book is available from the British Library.

Printed in Europe
Paper made from wood grown in sustainable forests and other controlled sources

1 3 5 7 9 10 8 6 4 2

www.scholastic.co.uk

The Bunny
Who
Came to
Breakfast

Rachael Davis

Mike Byrne

SCHOLASTIC

I want to share a special tale that started with a bushy tail.

One morning something made me **jump**,
I heard a pounding . . .

thump,
thump,
THUMP!

Then through the door
I saw a **paw,**

a wicker basket
made of straw,

two **large**
front teeth,
a **button nose,**

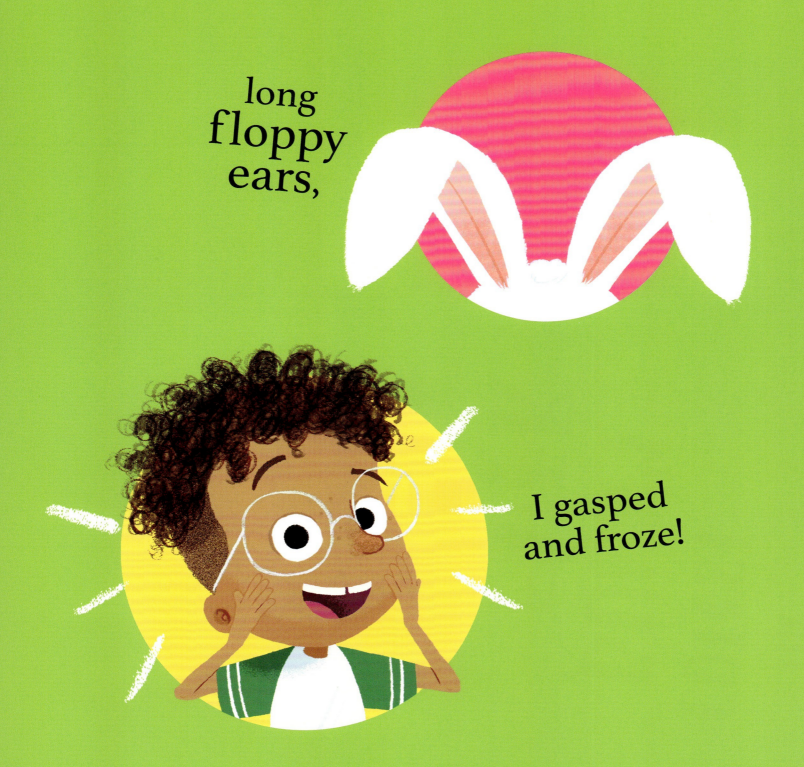

long
floppy
ears,

I gasped
and froze!

Now, can **you** guess what these **clues** mean?

THE CUTEST **BUNNY** **EVER** SEEN!

"Cooee," she sang, "It's only me,
oh, look at that nice pot of tea,
and, ooh, is that fresh bread I smell?
I'd love some breakfast - can you tell?"

"Please take a seat," my grandad said
and passed the jam and chocolate spread.
I sat with Bunny, still in awe,
and watched as she ate more and more.

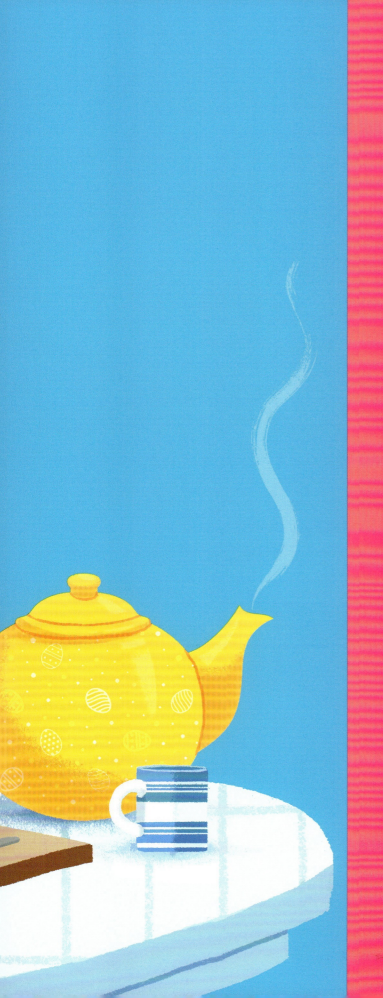

She gnawed a carrot,

MUNCH,
CRUNCH,
CRUNCH!

"You don't mind if I eat the bunch?"
Then perching on her strong hind legs,
she squeaked,
"Could I please have some...EGGS?!"

She ate them **scrambled**, **poached** and **fried**, cooked **upside down** and **sunny side**.

Next up was **omelette**, packed with cheese,

"Oh, just a few more, if you please. It's really boiled eggs I love most with runny yolks and dippy toast!"

Then through the window, Bunny spied . . .

My trampoline,
and smiling cried,
"Oh, please could I
have one quick go?
(I am an expert,
don't you know.)"

So, Bunny **bounded**
through the gate
and started jumping . . .

"This is great!"

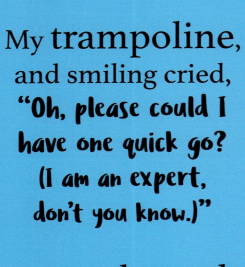

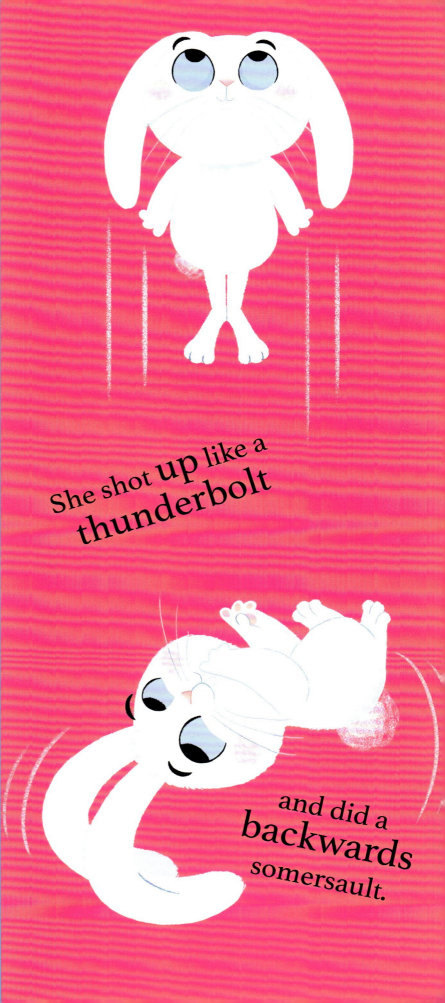

She shot up like a **thunderbolt**

and did a
backwards somersault.

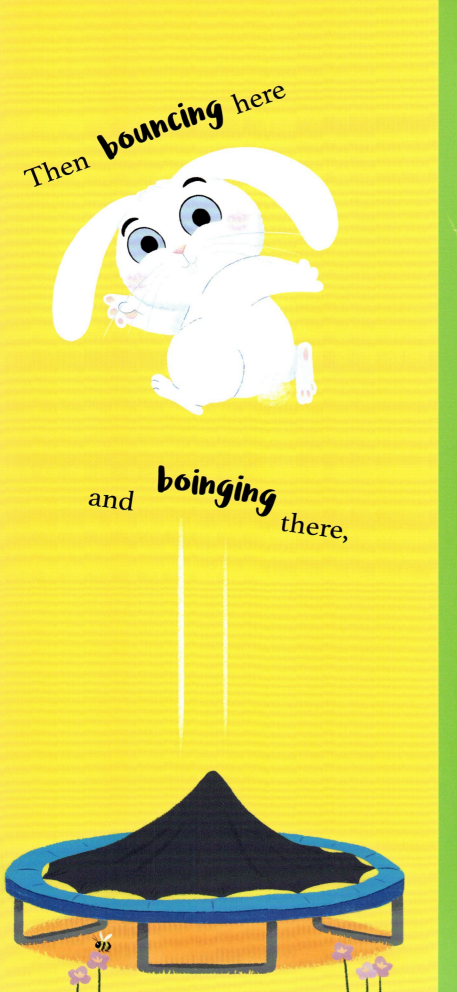

Then **bouncing** here

and **boinging** there,

soon she was **hopping** everywhere!

Then Bunny gave a **mighty** sniff,
her whiskers twitched,

"I've caught a whiff . . ."

She raced off to the chicken coop,
"I KNEW it!" Bunny gave a WHOOP
and grinned from floppy ear to ear.

"It's not JUST chicken eggs in here . . .

"It's chocolate eggs!"
"Oh, LOOK! Here's one!"

"An egg hunt!"
Bunny cheered,
"What fun!"

Each new egg was a pure delight,
a mix of dark choc,
milk and white.

Some big, some small,
some wrapped up well,
some solid with a sugar shell,
while others hollow,
full of sweets!

Soon Bunny's basket
filled with treats!

Then Bunny said, "I'd love a munch,
shall we go back and have some brunch?"

This day was **better** than I **dreamed.**
"Ah, there you are," my grandad beamed.

He mixed plain flour,
eggs and milk
and whisked the batter
smooth as silk.

The hot pan made a **sizzling** sound
as pancakes formed, all cute and round.

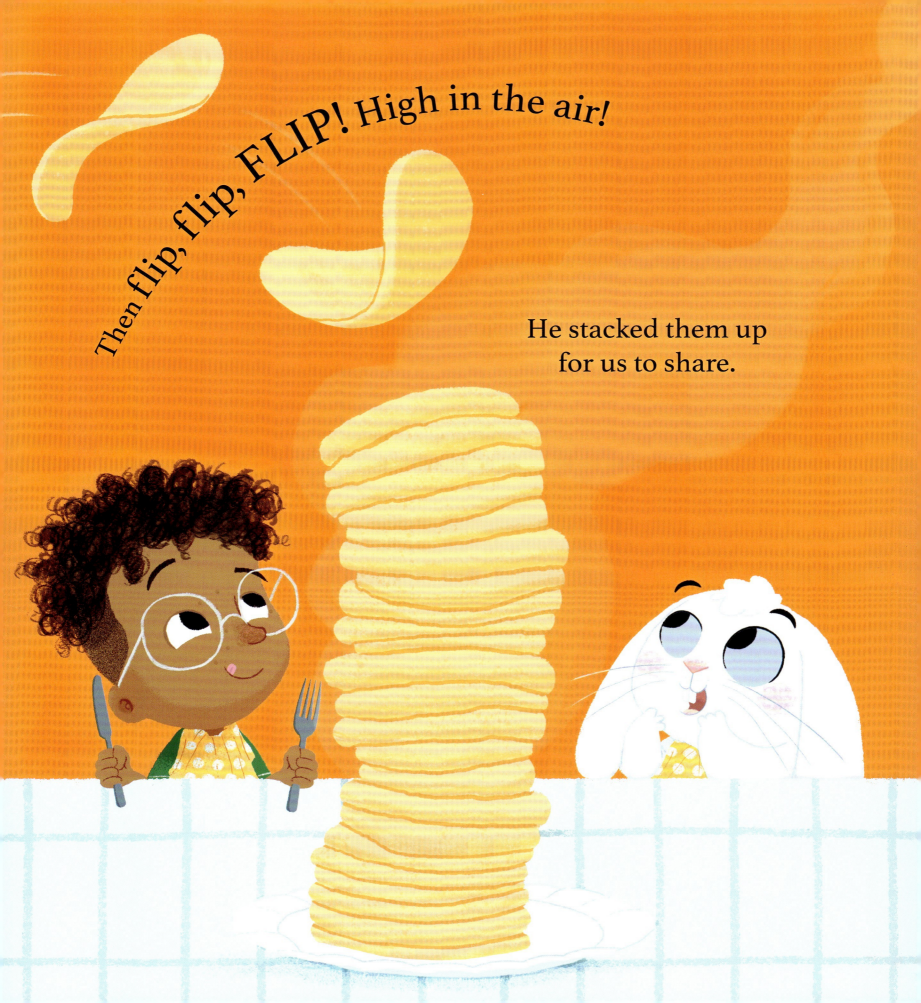

We **dived** straight in, toppings **galore**,

red berries, **nuts**, whipped cream and more.

From **sugar** with sharp **lemon** juice,

to ice
cream

and rich
chocolate
mousse.

Then Bunny gave a toothy grin,

"I love my pancakes covered in . . .
crisp streaky bacon – and the sauce?
Sweet maple syrup, please, of course!
With fresh fruit salad, if I may
(I like to get my five-a-day)."

Then Bunny licked her furry lips
"I'm stuffed" she cried, with hands on hips,
"Although perhaps just one last treat...
I'd love a special cake to eat!"

So, Grandad brought us crunchy flakes
and melted chocolate to make cakes.

We ate.

We danced.

We hopped

and bopped

(until we were so tired,
we flopped)!

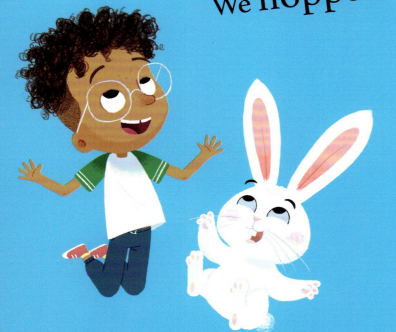

"Thanks," Bunny said,
"I must be off,
but please, just one
more egg to scoff."

We waved,
"**Please come
again to play**,
it's been the **most**
egg-citing day!"